PAUL JARVIS

BRITISH AIRWAYS
COLOURING BOOK

In association with **BRITISH AIRWAYS**

AMBERLEY

Opposite: This graphic clearly captures the new British Airways' size and the diversity of its aircraft fleet. It also highlights British Airways' need to get to grips quickly with the complexity of its operations if it was to be the success it was set up to be. With twelve aircraft types, from the supersonic Concorde to helicopters, and with as many different engine types again, in engineering terms alone such a diverse operation would be a major exercise to manage efficiently, profitably and, above all, safely – the number-one consideration for the new company.

First published 2016

Amberley Publishing
The Hill, Stroud
Gloucestershire, GL5 4EP

www.amberley-books.com

Line drawings digitally produced from work provided by the British Airways Museum.

ISBN 978 1 4456 6612 9 (print)

Typesetting by Amberley Publishing.
Printed in the UK.

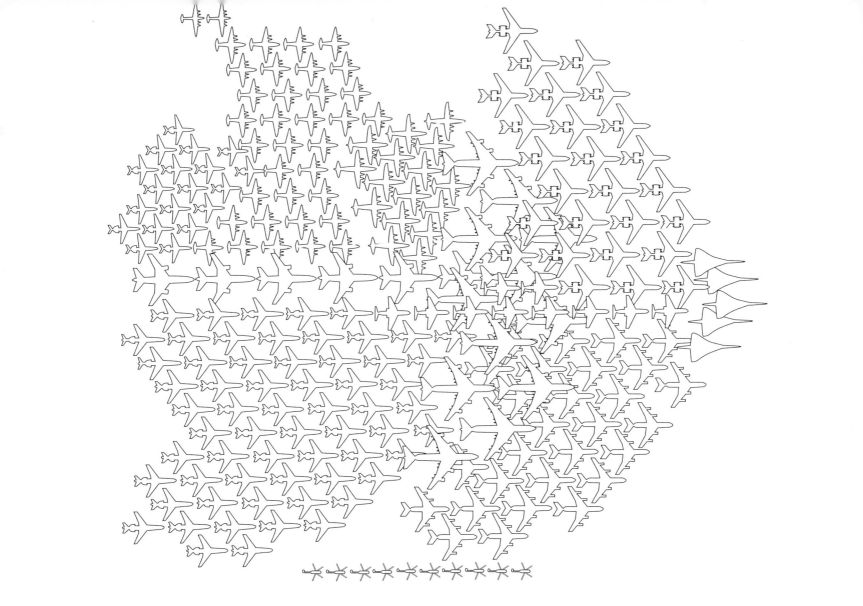

In 1975, the British Airways Board was granted a coat of arms and a motto – 'To Fly. To Serve' – and this was also used by British Airways. It was similar to BOAC's, not from any leaning towards its predecessor but because its make-up represented a much wider operation across the world. Simply put, on the new battlefield that international commercial aviation was to become in the final decades of the twentieth century, British Airways and its new livery would stand out and its motto, 'To Fly. To Serve', would be the standard around which its staff and loyal customers would rally.

TO FLY. TO SERVE

Comfort in the air, 1931 style. The scene could almost be from a railway or shipping brochure, both modes of transport serious competitors even for short European journeys. Airline standards of service were a consideration for many wealthy short-haul passengers when deciding which way to travel. (Tom Purvis)

The New Road to The East, a promotional brochure designed for Imperial Airways to promote its new services to India.
(Charles C. Dickson)

1920s traditionalism versus 1930s modernism: another example of Imperial's ageing fleet in contrast to the modern Luft Hansa monoplane taking off from Croydon. (Kenneth A. McDonough)

Although never implemented, the interior design for BOAC's abortive Avro Tudor was very forward-looking, with the use of brighter colours and a style that would do credit to the 1970s. The modern design reflected the work of BOAC's new design committee, industrial designer Richard Lonsdale-Hands and the influence of designer F. H. K. Henrion, who was engaged as the committee's consultant. (R. Lonsdale-Hands/J. Tandy)

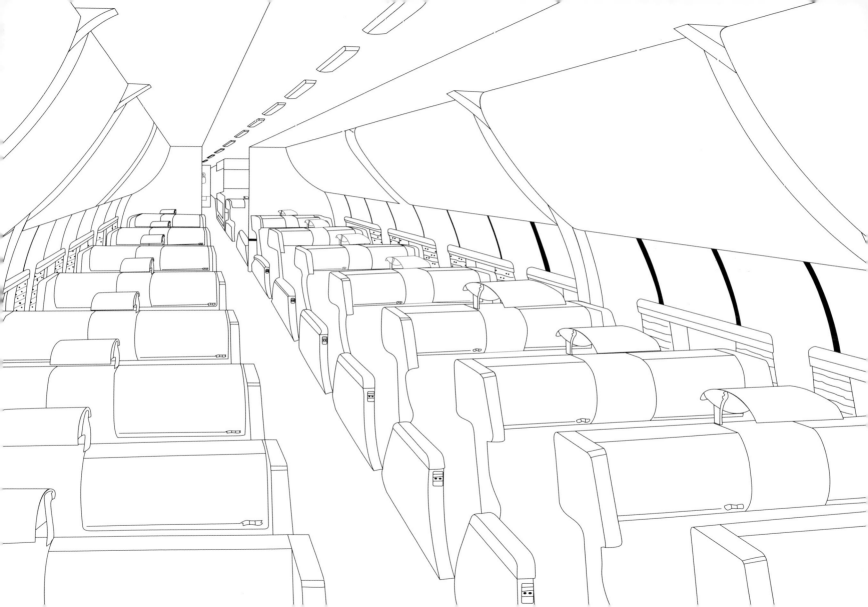

BOAC and South African Airways jointly advertised the UK–South Africa route in the late 1940s, sharing the revenue under a commercial 'pooling' agreement, a common arrangement in the early days of route development between two countries that had single international state airlines.

Fast but flawed. Three Comets fly in formation as part of an early promotional shoot for BOAC.

The Viscount had very high passenger appeal, with its quiet cabin and large picture windows offering excellent views; promotions of the time often featured these attractions.

'Swift, Silent, Serene.' BOAC's advertising capitalised on the VC10's quiet cabin, a result of placing the engines at the rear of the fuselage. (Frank Wootton)

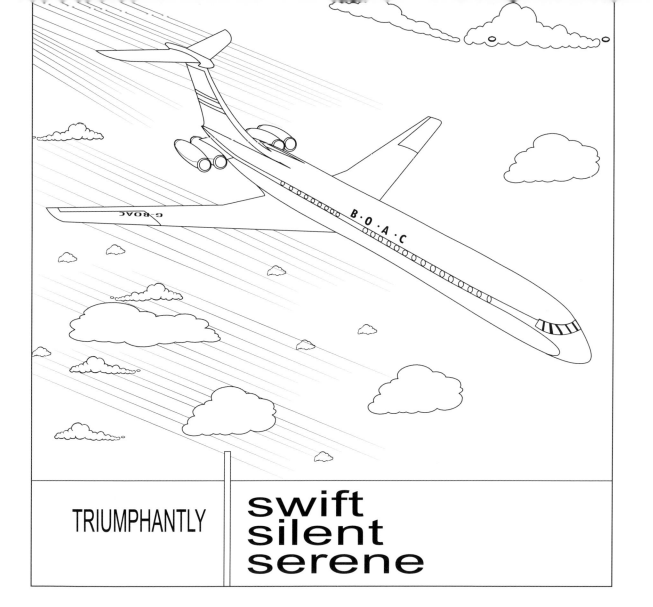

TRIUMPHANTLY

**swift
silent
serene**

The Hawker Siddeley Trident became the mainstay of the BEA fleet in the later 1960s and early 1970s and performed the world's first fully automated landing on a commercial service in summer 1965, a major technological advance for operations in poor visibility. The later variant, the Trident Three, was not BEA's first choice, however; they preferred the new Boeing 727, which had better operating costs and delivery options. The UK government vetoed the 727 to protect Hawker Siddeley, effectively increasing BEA's costs by several million pounds.

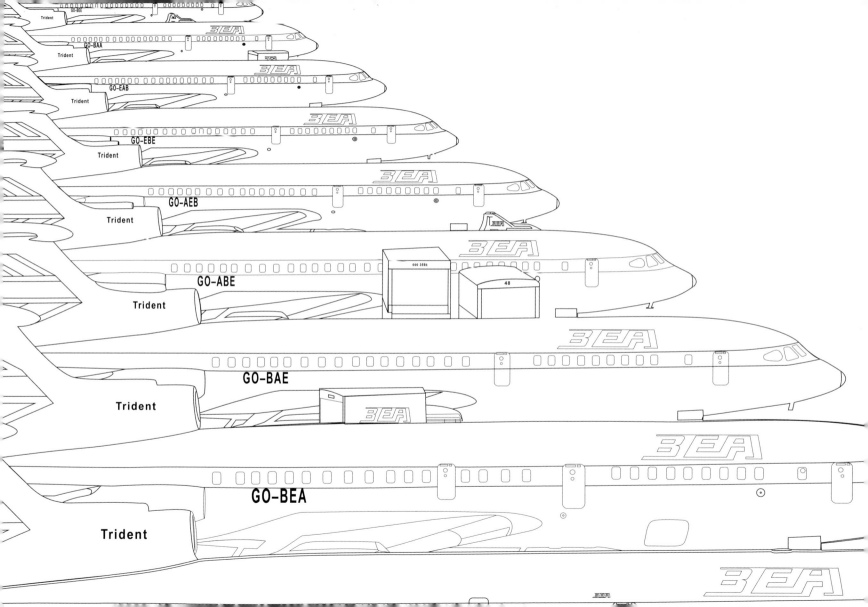

BEA Airtours operated a fleet of nine Comet 4Bs between the UK and various Mediterranean sunspots. In 1974 it became a wholly owned subsidiary of British Airways and was renamed British Airtours. It was again renamed in 1988 as Caledonian Airways following the acquisition of BCAL.

Although British Airways had to make substantial cuts across its business as part of its survival plan, its focus on customer service was not lost. The very successful 'Club' concept was further enhanced in 1981 by a 'Super Club' service on UK–USA routes, a super standard to supersede old Club and again take it above the competition. The new 'Expanda' seats were wider than many airlines' first-class seats and at six-abreast on US routes were an industry leader, with a middle seat that converted to a table.

From Concorde to the BAC 1-11, all BA's fleet types in the new Landor livery.

CONCORDE

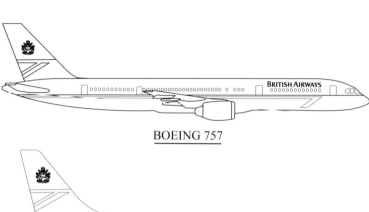

BOEING 757

BOEING 747

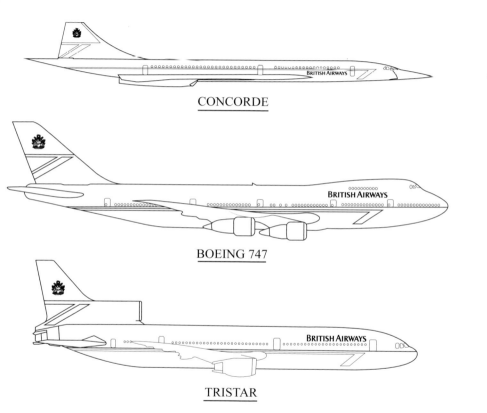

TRISTAR

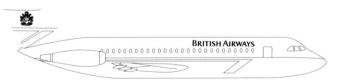

BOEING 737

BAC 1-11

A new livery complemented by a new uniform. Designed by the French couturier Roland Klein, British Airways' new uniform was stylish and of its time. The 'deckchair pattern', as it affectionately became known, was at once flattering and flattening. Drape shoulders and straight skirts suited some but not all, but that was the 1980s!

'Britain's highest flying company': issued as part of the flotation as an explanatory document on British Airways, the public did not need a glossy brochure to know a good deal when they saw one. Eleven times oversubscribed, British Airways staff also piled in, with 94 per cent of them taking shares and a direct financial interest in the company's performance.

TO FLY TO SERVE

BRITISH AIRWAYS
The world's favourite airline.

A British Airways Ltd Fokker F.XII about to depart from Gatwick's Martello Terminal in 1936. (Kenneth A. McDonough)

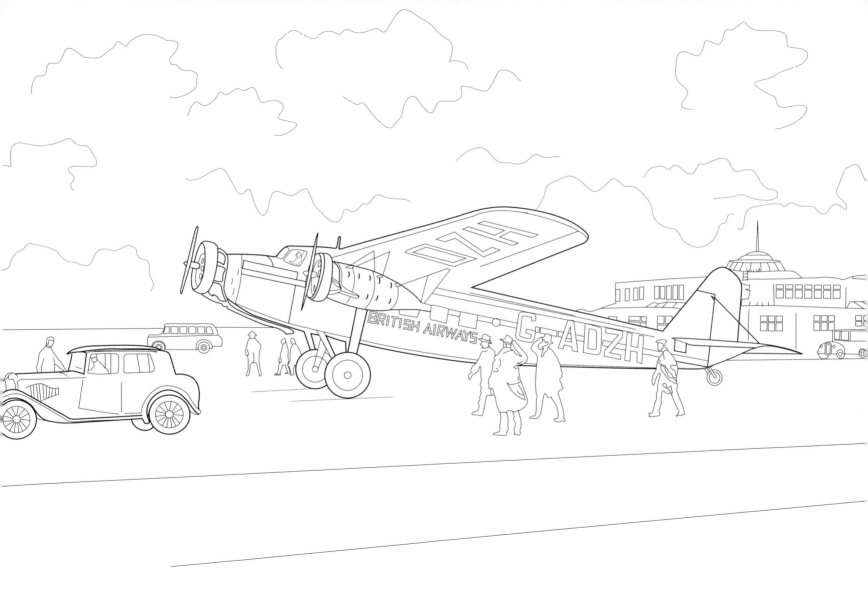

An attractive in-flight menu for one of British Airways' new World Traveller services to the Middle East, which includes a small quiz. (Maggie Kneen)

WHERE IN THE WORLD?

This picture contains 10 clues that will reveal a British Airways World Traveller destination.

Can you identify the destination?

Can you spot all 10 clues?

For the answer, see inside this menu.

BRITISH AIRWAYS

British Airways' new advertising campaign, called 'Global', was launched worldwide in early 1990 and became an instant hit, winning several major awards. An endearing use of hundreds of people in coloured costumes creating happy faces, it was intended to communicate the caring and friendly characteristics of British Airways' staff and emphasise the size of the airline's network. (Saatchi & Saatchi)

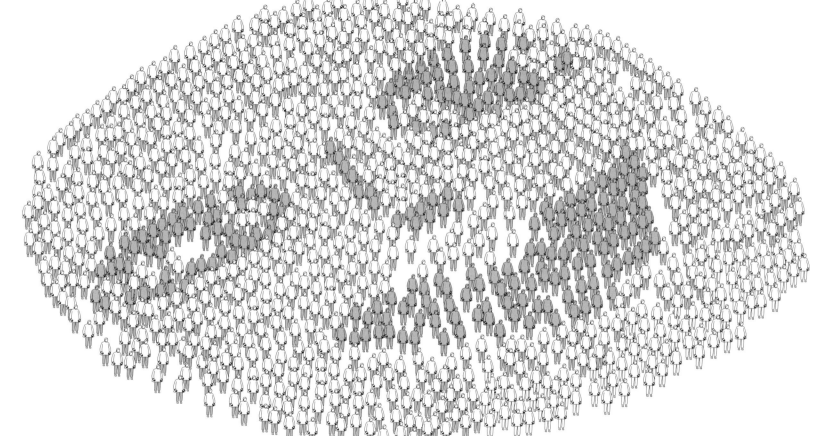

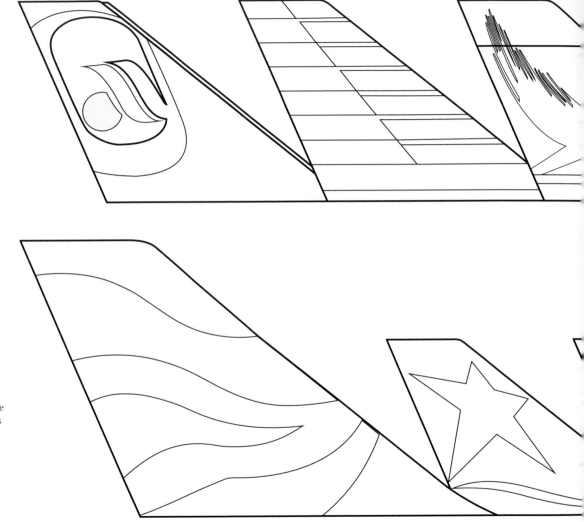

By 2013, the oneworld alliance had grown to twelve full members, with twenty-two affiliated members and three members elect, including USAirways following its merger with American Airlines.

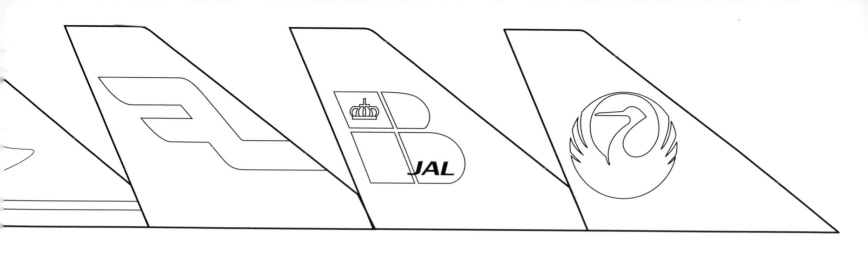

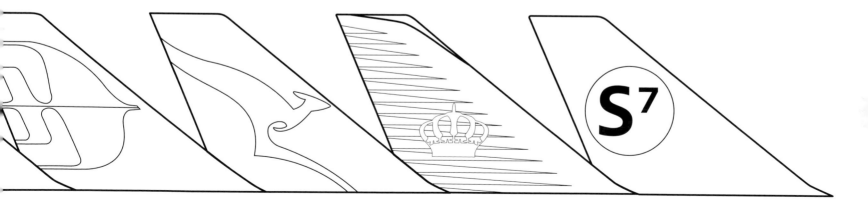

Following the terrorist attack on the World Trade Centre in New York, all US domestic and international flights to and from the USA were grounded for several days. Services resumed but with enhanced security measures that caused serious delays and still reverberate around the operation of all air services worldwide.

Six British Airways Concordes now grace museums in the UK and abroad and the seventh remains at Heathrow. Alpha Foxtrot resides at Filton near Bristol, here seen passing over Brunel's iconic suspension bridge in a salute to nineteenth- and twentieth-century technological innovation. (South West News Service)

Concorde returned to service in 2001 but had suffered badly from the serious reduction in business traffic following the 11 September attack. Her retirement in October 2003 saw the end of the commercial supersonic era. It was a sad farewell but the time machine had reached its final destination.

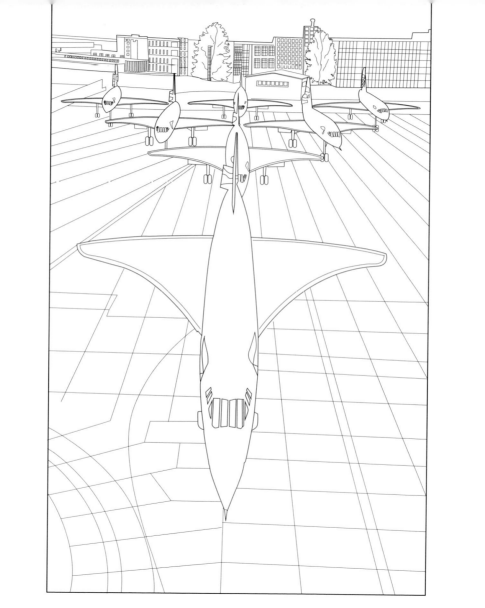

British Airways' report to shareholders in November 2010 filled in the missing piece in British Airways' globalisation jigsaw.

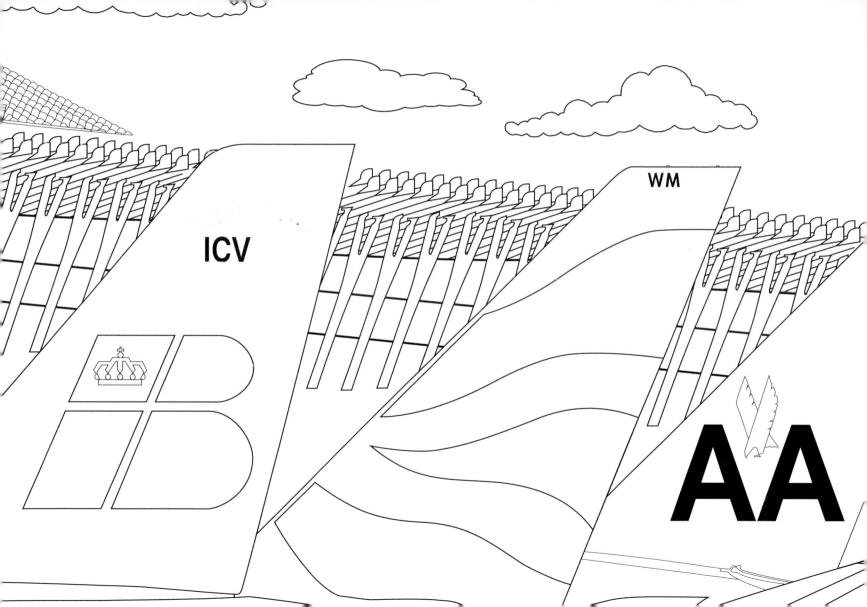

Concorde's flight numbers BA001 and BA003 were reintroduced for the inauguration of the first London to New York services out of London City Airport. Using an Airbus A318 aircraft with a thirty-two-seat, all-business configuration, the flight refuels in Shannon, where US customs and immigration clearances are completed, allowing customers to depart quickly on arrival in New York. (Nick Morrish)

British Airways' 2012 advertising also included a very successful 'Don't Fly' campaign to encourage visitors to the London 2012 Olympics and Paralympic Games. (Bartle Bogle Hegarty)

The Boeing 787-8 Dreamliner is something else again, technologically ultra-modern in its construction, mainly of composite materials, and with twenty-first-century styling for the aircraft's interior.

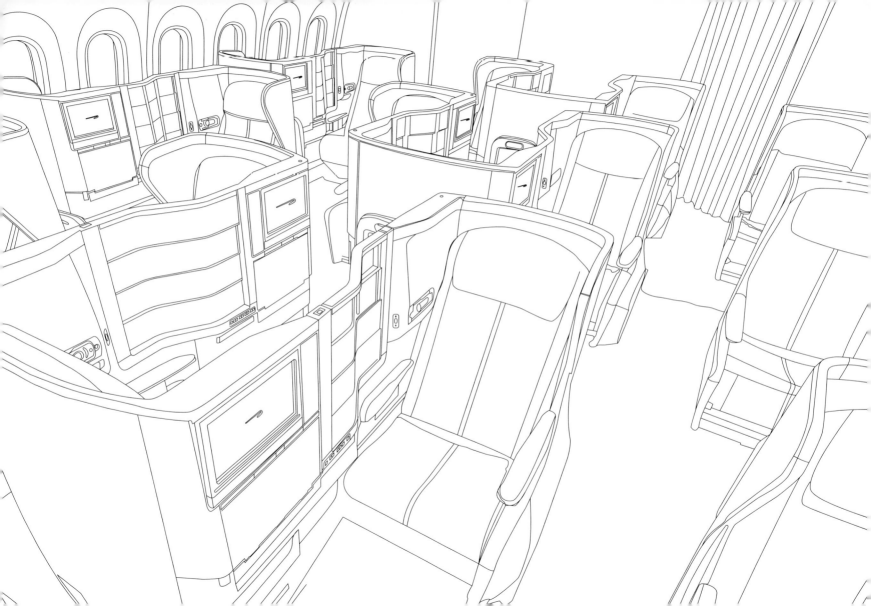

This Imperial Airways poster from the mid-1930s could be described as a very simplified map, but the points of origin and destination of the journey are probably meant to be incidental to the main thrust and dynamism of the image emphasising both the speed and the implied safety and comfort of Imperial's four-engined De Havilland 86 aircraft. To reach Australia in only ten and a half days was a marvel in the 1930s, the only alternative being over a month by ship. The aircraft shown in the poster is actually registered to Qantas, the then Australian national airline, with which Imperial operated a joint service carrying the passengers to Singapore, then part of the British Empire, and transferring them to Qantas for the final part of the journey to Darwin and beyond. Ten and a half days is also a rather creative way of emphasising the speed of the journey – that was only the time it would take to reach Darwin. To go on to Brisbane or Sydney would take another one and a half or two and a half days respectively. (Brenet)

IMPERIAL AIRWAYS

AND ASSOCIATED COMPANIES

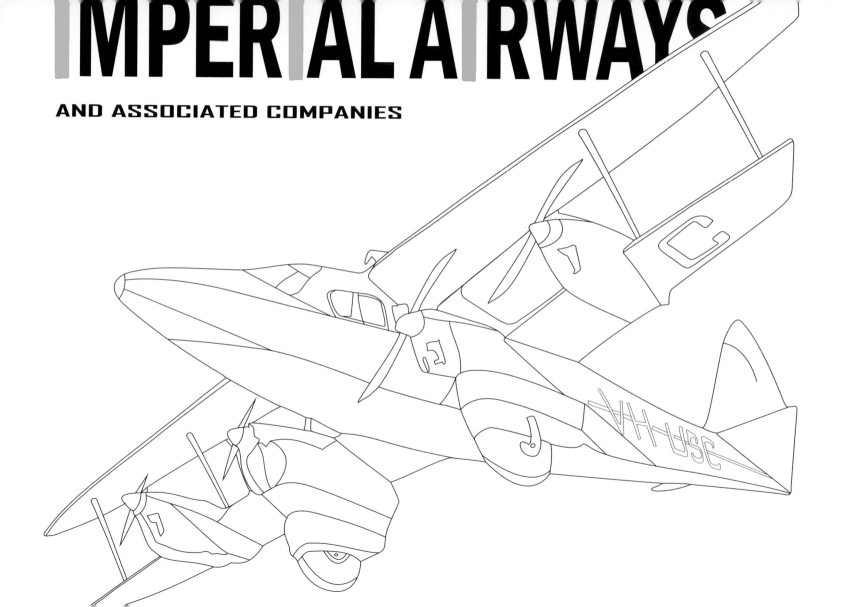

The Speedbird logo was not used on aircraft until 1939 as Imperial's management took the view it was not appropriate to decorate its rather austere aircraft livery of pale grey with a stylistic symbol. (Theyre Lee-Elliott)

By contrast with its European promotions, Imperial Airways had all the mystery and allure of the far-flung places of the British Empire with which to embellish its long-haul overseas advertising. Using all the skills and imagination of its agency creatives, Imperial produced many stylised and detailed factual and artistic representations of the world routes and places that it served and the aircraft it operated. Imperial also used many quite simple, purely informative geographical maps and diagrammatic illustrations. For Imperial's long-haul services with many stops en route, a diagrammatic map made a lot of sense in clarifying the route to be taken and the places served.

Le Touquet was hardly a European capital but it was an important destination for Imperial's well-heeled customers wishing to take a weekend break on the French coast and sample the delights, or frustrations, of the casinos and local golf courses. The sandy beaches were pretty good too.

6 P.M. IN LONDON

7.45 P.M. IN LE TOUQUET

and this includes tea at the
Casino and dinner in the air
on your return flight

An interesting piece of promotional artistry depicting Imperial Airways' new fleets of land and sea planes, ordered as a result of the introduction of the GPO's Empire Air Mail scheme.

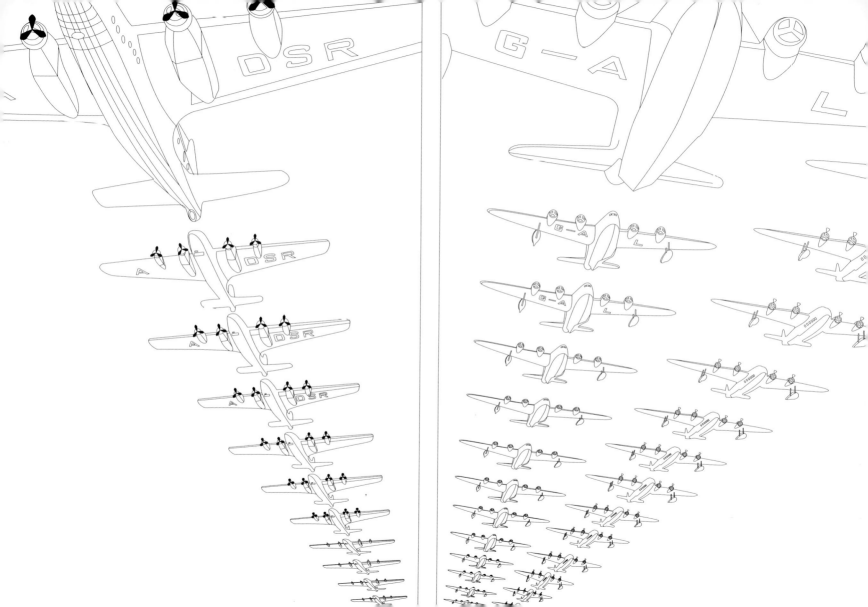

Just to explain what a Vickers Viking looks like, BEA often issued quite detailed cutaway promotional material of its aircraft types to show the interior layout and emphasise their 'luxury travel'. It was certainly not luxury by modern standards, but in the context of the time a huge advance in just ten years since the latter days of Imperial Airways.

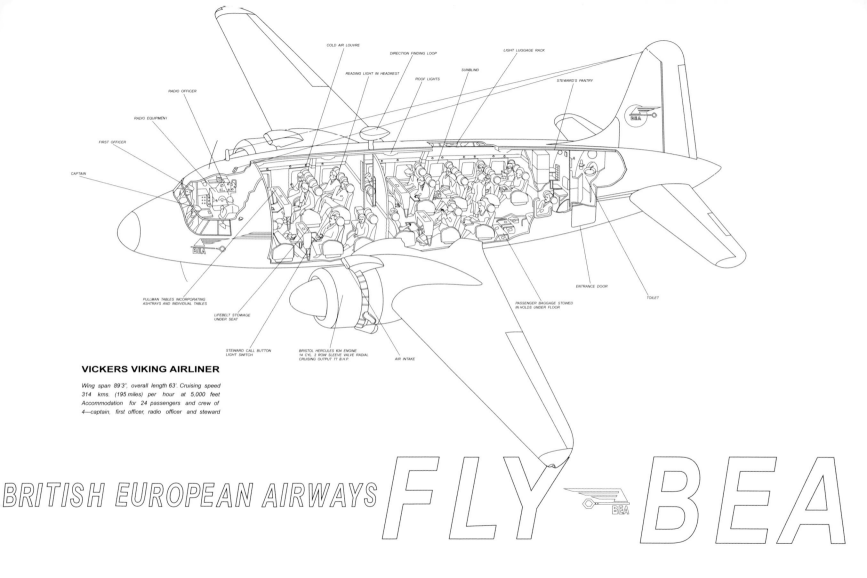

COLD AIR LOUVRE

DIRECTION FINDING LOOP

READING LIGHT IN HEADREST

LIGHT LUGGAGE RACK

ROOF LIGHTS

SUNBLIND

STEWARD'S PANTRY

RADIO OFFICER

RADIO EQUIPMENT

FIRST OFFICER

CAPTAIN

PULLMAN TABLES INCORPORATING
ASHTRAYS AND INDIVIDUAL TABLES

LIFEBELT STOWAGE
UNDER SEAT

STEWARD CALL BUTTON
LIGHT SWITCH

BRISTOL HERCULES 634 ENGINE
14 CYL. 2 ROW SLEEVE VALVE RADIAL
CRUISING OUTPUT 77 B.H.P.

AIR INTAKE

ENTRANCE DOOR

TOILET

PASSENGER BAGGAGE STOWED
IN HOLDS UNDER FLOOR

VICKERS VIKING AIRLINER

*Wing span 89'3", overall length 63'. Cruising speed
314 kms. (195 miles) per hour at 5,000 feet
Accommodation for 24 passengers and crew of
4—captain, first officer, radio officer and steward*

BRITISH EUROPEAN AIRWAYS FLY-BEA

BOAC did continue, here and there, the use of maps as promotional mediums where they had a direct impact and not just as decoration. This late 1960s timetable map is quite different from the geography book versions that had been used for some years, adding a distinct style and interest to a solid, standard Mercator's projection of the world overlaid on what might be considered turbulent oceans. What is also striking is the spread of BOAC's route network. It certainly spanned all six continents and to an extent more significant than earlier years, albeit the Polar and Siberian routes had yet to be authorised and there was still a distinct lack of depth in routes to South America. It also predates the loss of the lucrative West African and Saudi Arabian routes licences that were subsequently taken by the UK government and given to help the UK's up-and-coming 'second force' airline, British Caledonian Airways.

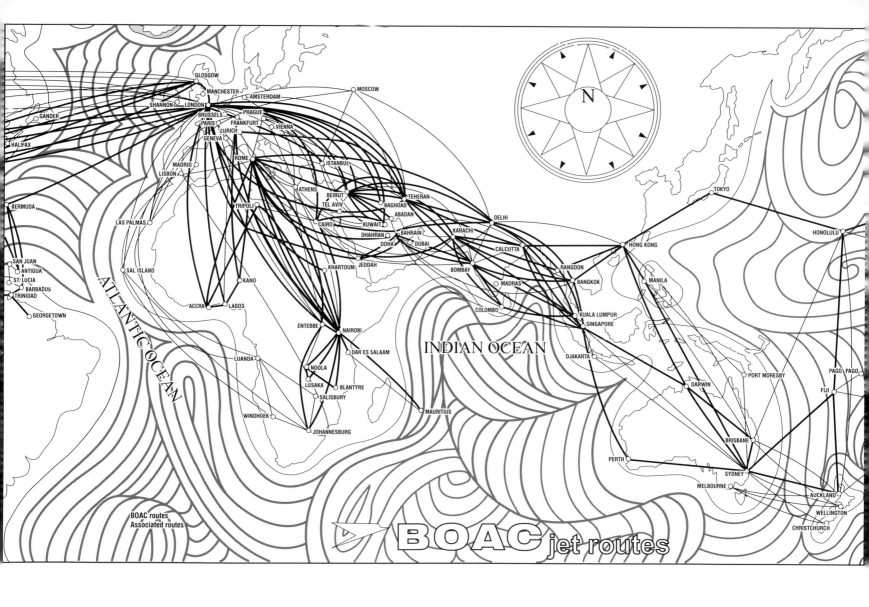

During the early 1950s, new, modern aircraft joined the fleets of both BOAC and BEA. They gave the opportunity for both airlines to develop their own distinctive on-board services and products, e.g. BOAC's 'Monarch' service on its North Atlantic routes and 'Majestic' service elsewhere.

BOAC's Monarch first-class customers on their luxury Stratocruiser aircraft had no on-board service limitations. They even had a lower-deck club lounge to relax in and enjoy a free canapé and cocktail while awaiting the preparation of a personally served dinner of Turtle Soup Royale followed by Filet Mignon and fine wines.

TAKES GOOD CARE OF YOU

A serious rival to the 707 was the British-built Vickers VC10 aircraft. It could not quite match the 707's economic performance but more than made up for that in passenger appeal. This was BOAC's chance to stand out from the crowd, and it certainly made a glamorous attempt. Advertised as 'Swift, Silent, Serene' due to the engines being placed at the rear of the aircraft, it promised matchless comfort 'in the most comfortable economy class seat in the world'. Superior cabin style and comfort was one way to get around the industry agreements limiting what could be offered to economy passengers. A revolutionary new seat with facings by the British designer Robin Day increased legroom and gave more overall space. Although the industry rules limited the distance between economy seats, nothing was said about the design of the seat or the design of the aircraft cabin. This was an opportunity BOAC exploited to the full, with an interior design by Day's wife, the renowned interior designer Lucienne Day.

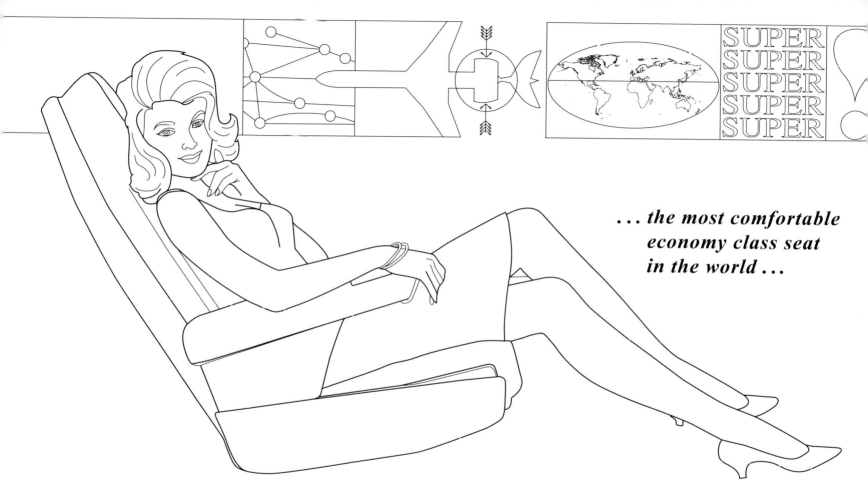

... the most comfortable
economy class seat
in the world ...

sitting pretty aboard the BOAC VC10

By the early 1970s, price innovation coupled with exotic destinations were encouraging more and more people to fly. BOAC's low-cost advance booking fares and inclusive tour holidays were packaged under the name 'Earthshrinkers'. The earth was certainly shrinking by the early 1970s as lower air fares began to encourage many people in the Western world to think globally when making their holiday travel plans. There was a widespread use of cartoon characters and graphics in the 1970s, a sort of 'pop art', extroverted approach following their use in commercial brand advertising from the 1960s onwards and instant appeal to the younger consumer. This was a particular target market for BOAC, with the expectation that it would be this consumer group with increasing disposable income that would be interested in travelling farther afield for their holidays.

we'll give you 15 days in East Africa.

Take a BOAC Earthshrinker holiday for £153.

Fly-Cruise Winter holidays were a new idea that packaged the ease of flying in a few hours to the sunshine of the Caribbean and transferring to a luxury ship to cruise the islands. Chandris Cruises' passenger liner *Romanza* looks more 1930s than 1970s which, indeed, she was, having been built in 1939 and, after only one voyage, taken over by the German navy as a repair vessel during the Second World War. Looking outdated compared to the ultra-modern Caribbean cruise liners of later years, she nevertheless has an old-world charm about her that must have made such cruises very enjoyable for her passengers. BOAC's VC10 aircraft shown on the brochure cover flew passengers to Antigua to embark on the *Romanza* or her sister ship *Regina* for a fifteen-day cruise from £194 per person, all-inclusive.

'Flying more people to more countries' was an advertising story used in the 1960s and early 1970s by BEA and was the basis of BEA's claim to be 'No. 1 in Europe'. The strapline worked well for BEA, so why not British Airways? And so it did, being used extensively and successfully from 1983 for many years in conjunction with the accolade of 'the World's Favourite Airline'. (This page: Saatchi & Saatchi)

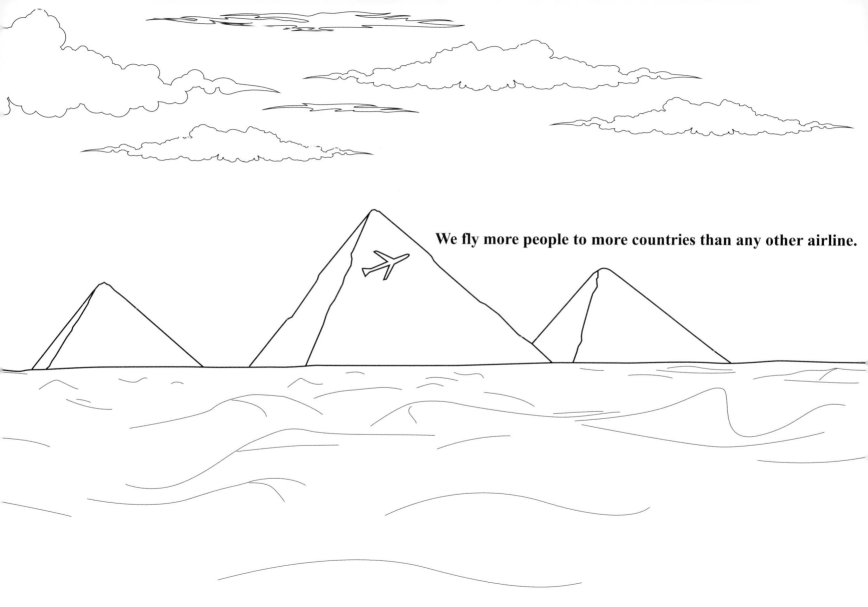

We fly more people to more countries than any other airline.

The traditional rock painting art of the Ncoakhoe tribe of the San people of the Kalahari Desert by the artist Cgoise, one of five women in a group of tribal artists working out of the Kuru Development Trust, an indigenous organisation for the self-development of the San people. This artwork can be seen in British Airways' headquarters building at Harmondsworth, near Heathrow. (Cgoise)

In the mid-1950s, BOAC introduced national dress uniforms for its Chinese, Indian, Pakistani and Japanese services. White cheongsams, colourful saris and traditional kimonos were worn by national stewardesses from these countries who spoke the relevant languages and understood the associated cultures. It was an extension of BOAC's 'taking more care' approach on routes with which it had strong historic links, and it was a service enhancement much appreciated by passengers.

On the Trans-Pacific Routes, Japanese and
Chinese stewardesses add a charm and courtesy of their
own to the golden legend of B.O.A.C. cabin service.

In 1969 BOAC had taken delivery of its first 747 aircraft and also introduced an entirely new uniform. Up-and-coming British designer Clive Evans had done well to win the tender from Mary Quant and Jean Muir, both leading UK designers of 1960s fashion. Clive's new uniform was certainly very different from its predecessor and very much reflected both practicality and the new 'London Look'. The theme of practicality first and fashion second had by now become the defining approach to BOAC's (and BEA's) uniform designs. With much greater numbers of passengers on the 747 and the demands of both Arctic winds and tropical steam heat, the uniform ensemble certainly needed to be practical but also needed to look good and be aligned to the fashion of the time. The summer uniform in Caribbean blue or coral pink was certainly easy-wear and practical, being made from terylene and cotton twill, and was washable in a hotel sink to drip-dry overnight. The winter dress and jacket in terylene and wool worsted was also easy-care and stayed immaculate whatever the weather threw at it.

BOAC stewardesses world-wide will
wear the new uniform, which makes its first
appearance aboard the BOAC 747

Julien Macdonald certainly has a couture pedigree as former artistic director for the House of Givenchy in Paris and head knitwear designer at Chanel. His designs are highly sophisticated, glamorous and elegant and he has applied the same philosophy to the current British Airways uniform, resulting in a sharp, modern silhouette with a respectful nod to its heritage. Female cabin crew have a choice of wearing skirts or trousers in a navy pinstripe wool fabric, complemented by a white blouse with red detailing and a bespoke patterned cravat worn under a smart fitted jacket with silver buttons. Celebrated British milliner Stephen Jones designed the hat. The male and female flight crew uniforms continue the trend introduced by Roland Klein for silver braid rank markings that rather emphasise that cool assurance and 'dash' that only a uniform can imply.

British Airways' website, ba.com, has rapidly become the single biggest contact point for its customers worldwide, one of the most sophisticated internet travel sites and a key component of its brand promise. The occasional difficulties of checking in have been transformed online – 'rarely is check-in as quiet as a mouse'. (Bartle Bogle Hegarty)

If only packing
was as simple
as checking in
from home.

ba.com

Just ahead of the formation of IAG was the announcement of regulatory clearance for the long-awaited Atlantic alliance between British Airways, American Airlines and Iberia. This was all about linking the combined strengths of the three airlines to offer major improvements in customer benefits, over 1,000 flat beds a day between London and New York in 2014 being a notable example. It would not change the look and feel of each airline's brand, and no aircraft would be painted in the advert's rather fanciful montage, but it would be a major improvement to the ease with which customers could travel across the three airlines' combined networks, almost as if they were one airline.

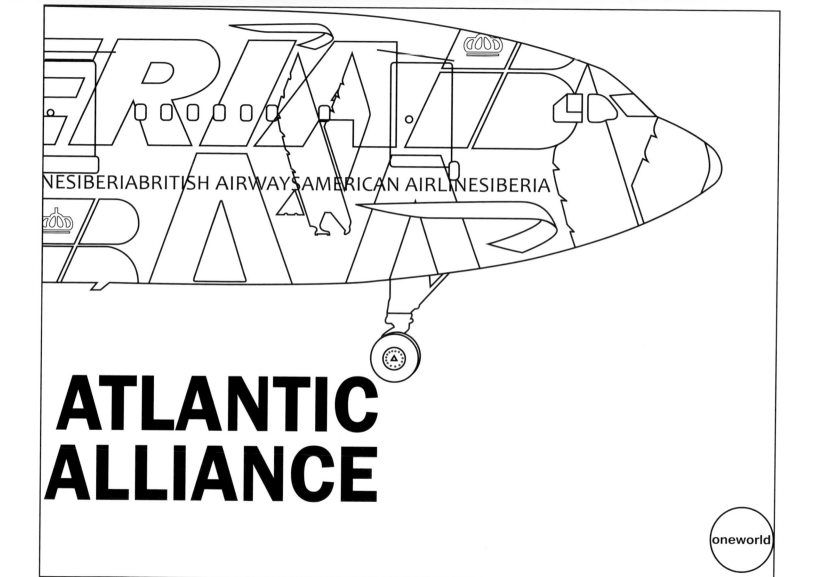

NESIBERIABRITISH AIRWAYSAMERICAN AIRLINESIBERIA

ATLANTIC ALLIANCE

oneworld

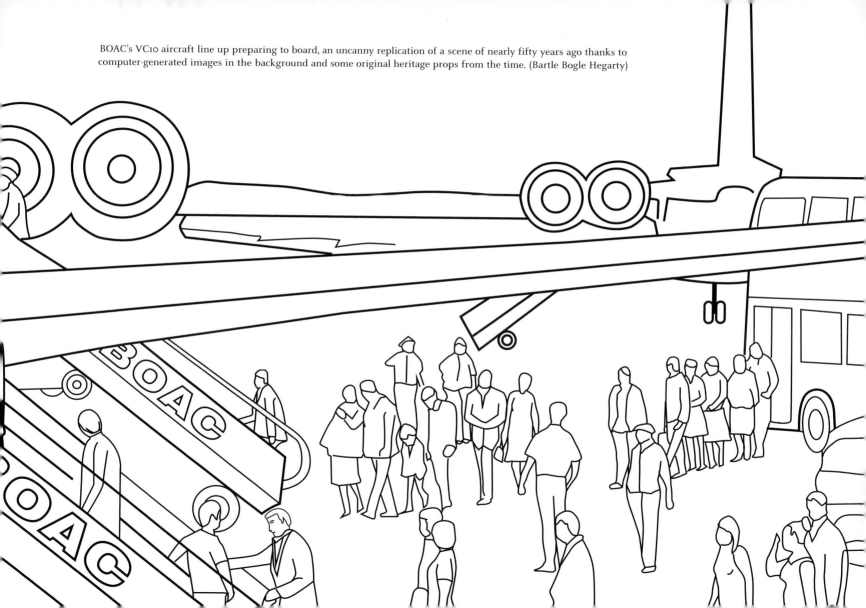

BOAC's VC10 aircraft line up preparing to board, an uncanny replication of a scene of nearly fifty years ago thanks to computer-generated images in the background and some original heritage props from the time. (Bartle Bogle Hegarty)

'To Fly. To Serve.' is now the consistent manifestation of the airline's brand promise to perform, a simple message that clearly says what British Airways and its people stand for in putting their customers at the heart of their business. 'Welcome to British Airways.'

BRITISH AIRWAYS

To invest.
To add to our fleet.
To feel at home at 39.000ft.

With our new A380 and
Boeing 787 Dreamiliners,
expect even more comfort
than ever before.

To Fly. To Serve.

oneworld